Praise for Quintin Collins

"Reading *Claim Tickets for Stolen People* creates the feeling one has studying a transcendental sonogram: Collins's poetry brings inner life into focus. Blackness is reclaimed, celebrated, embodied. He can give shape to Barack Obama's tan suit and Jimi Hendrix's guitar. He can be furious, funny, and fatherly in a single poem, with a range as broad as his compassion. This is a marvelous book. *Claim Tickets for Stolen People* gives shape to our magical, mercurial world."

   —Terrance Hayes

"*Claim Tickets for Stolen People* is an alternative history book in which Black storying, Black sayings, and Black mythology are the truest things we know. It is a new gospel that hones in on shared moments within Black experience—the sound of a radiator thundering at night, the sight of an uncle's chest hair silvering through his Figaro chain, the way sugar makes a home in the blood of our elders. With an archeologist's precision, Collins digs a Black truth from the soil of historical erasure, from the graves of those we have lost to white supremacist violence."

   —Taylor Byas

"*Claim Tickets for Stolen People* is that first sip of ice cold water on a summer day where the concrete sizzles. Collins's tight control of rhythm and language pop with vignettes that surprise while retaining the familiar scent of home. A quick-witted, empathetic consideration of the memories that make us."

   —Jeni De La O

"Collins' poetic vignettes delight in local vernacular, hang at street level, let us touch the dirt with our own hands such that we might feel, perhaps even understand, what it means to grow as the titular, undesirable weed. . . . By the end of this collection, we're not trying to root out the dandelion from our grounds but root for its continued resilience."

   —Cortney Lamar Charleston (on *The Dandelion Speaks of Survival*)

"While tenderness and joy abound in this promising debut, the most powerful moments see 'fresh to death' boys, posturing and vulnerable, trying to tear a way out of the social contradictions, mislaid hungers, and racial erasure swirling around them in an American warpland."

—Iain Haley Pollock (on *The Dandelion Speaks of Survival*)

"There should be a collective noun to describe Quintin Collins's poetry—a heat of poetry. Poem-to-poem, it's fierce and formidable, sensuous and hip."

—Dzvinia Orlowsky (on *The Dandelion Speaks of Survival*)

Claim Tickets for Stolen People

The Journal Charles B. Wheeler Poetry Prize

Claim Tickets for Stolen People

Quintin Collins

MAD CREEK BOOKS, AN IMPRINT OF
THE OHIO STATE UNIVERSITY PRESS
COLUMBUS

Library of Congress Cataloging-in-Publication Data
Names: Collins, Quintin, author.
Title: Claim tickets for stolen people / Quintin Collins.
Description: Columbus : Mad Creek Books, an imprint of The Ohio State University
    Press, [2022] | Series: *The Journal* Charles B. Wheeler Poetry Prize | Summary: "A
    collection of poems that celebrates and reimagines the power of Blackness in
    America"—Provided by publisher.
Identifiers: LCCN 2021035114 | ISBN 9780814258149 (paperback) | ISBN 081425814X
    (paperback) | ISBN 9780814281727 (ebook) | ISBN 0814281729 (ebook)
Subjects: LCGFT: Poetry.
Classification: LCC PS3603.O4548 C57 2022 | DDC 811/.6—dc23
LC record available at https://lccn.loc.gov/2021035114

Cover design by Derek Thornton
Text design by Juliet Williams
Type set in Capita and Rockwell

For Harper

Contents

Acknowledgments

Thank you to Daniel B. Summerhill, Jeni De La O, and Erin J. Bauman for their comments and support in bringing these poems to life and maturity. Also, many thanks to Marcus Jackson for believing in the work.

Thank you to each of the following publications where certain poems have appeared or are forthcoming in the current or earlier drafts:

Ghost City Review: "What Waves Will Carry Back to You"

Glass: A Journal of Poetry: "Delayed MBTA Train Home as Jimi Hendrix's Stratocaster"

Gumbo Media: "See What Had Happened Was"; "Kick Back on the Moon"

The Hellebore: "Reynolds-Wrapped Leftovers"

Homology Lit: "Black History Year"; "Obama's Tan Suit" (then titled "Claim Ticket 60615: Obama's Tan Suit"); "Samuel L. Jackson's 'Motherfucker'" (then titled "Claim Ticket 1221: Samuel L. Jackson's 'Motherfucker'")

Knight's Library Magazine: "Isaiah Bradley in Conversation with Barack Obama"

The Poet's Billow: "all-american black body"; "How We Work This Soil"

Pushcart Prize XLVI: "pluto be orbit uncommon"

Redivider: "Exegesis on a Chicken Wing"

Sidereal Magazine: "pluto be orbit uncommon"; "a summer lesson on multiplication"; "The Alchemy of Our Uncles' Chest Hair"

What Rough Beast: "Generation Snowflake"; "The Freedom Trail Tour Guide Shyly Mentions Slaves Were Sold at Boston Harbor"; "the bees rebuild"; "Would-Be Rats"

See What Had Happened Was

Storying means the "lies" black folks tell to
amuse themselves and to explain their origins.
—KEVIN YOUNG

Truth fidgeted into knots
—caught telling stories—
see what had happened was

—*I was on my way to*—
I had it when I left—
truth fidgeted into not

truth—I refashioned
myself—tongue tripped—
see what had happened was

I twisted and looped
truth—ancestors forged freedom
—truth fidgeted into knots

—throat a knot,
but don't I untangle narrative—
see what had happened was,

mama, teacher, officer—I'll story
a reality from here to Zion—
see what had happened was
I fidgeted truth out of nots.

This Life My Father Roused

My father, baptized by morning dew: he mows,
he trims, he sweeps, he bags. He shepherds

patio furniture into prayer circles. He exorcises
dust from chair cushions—heirlooms after funeral.

To another heirloom, his father's grill, he feeds coal
bellyfuls that go from smirks of ember to cackle of blaze.

He tong-turns hot dogs, hot links, chicken thighs,
burgers, ribs, and pork chops. He turns up the stereo

to woo the late arrivers. Aretha serenades her angel.
We thank God for everyone there, everyone not, every hand

that made the food, and the food. Sweet Baby Ray's sticky stains
and King's Hawaiian rolls butter-blessed, we commune

over two plates, Miller High Life, and then 7 Up cake
before a deck of cards smites the tabletop. Before fireworks,

this life my father roused at dawn with a lawnmower
full of gasoline. A boom trumpets the cookout,

but not illumination to celebrate independence—
my father's laughter, a rapture like a firecracker in twilight.

Watermelon Seed

Given our history, we could dive into water
only on land, feel the coolness on our faces
with no sharks in this sea. A baptism,
but no reverend or heaven to resurrect
life into our lungs. These waters flood
our cheekbones, juice in our dimples
—how we gnash the flesh to mush
like watermelon smashed against a rock.
Fruit devoured to rind, we collect a seed
between our lips, spit back the kernels
to earth. Speartips of melon
in our grip, we fling bits of life
off our fingernails, over the porch rail,
into the grass. The seeds wait for rain.

a summer lesson on multiplication

like these kids multiply
         at playgrounds after school lets out pinball children
bump &   red rover &   run & swing &   freeze
tag &   red light green light & simon says
        always more bodies baked   when sun sweats
high noon hits   always more sweat
always more children   more Huffy more Wilson
    thrown across Ravisloe Terrace & hollers these boys throw
    to girls teeth sucked   back at boys
more super soakers   sprinkler runs   always more summer
hours always more   kids at Atkins Park for more
wood mulch splinters   bomb pop popsicle sticks
      & kids seek freedom before they know freedom
   isn't   for them   freedom isn't   for them   freedom
a feat for daddy's   day off   miller high life cans
   barry white through speakers freedom a feat
      for momma to watch tv in bed all day
for momma & daddy   to kick kids out the house
     & don't come back for a few hours
just don't go too far & make sure you check in
   every hour as if these kids wear watches or watch
sun skip   then hop   through the hours
too busy multiplying on every block   little siblings
new to this but in tow &   cousins staying for summer
     & all these damn kids running
the block   more Mongoose   more Razor
   more Spalding   more *run it back*   more running back
before streetlight   more *i'm sorry mama* just a mistake
just broke neighbor's stoop light   neighbor's window
it wasn't me mama i swear it wasn't me   but law
      of multiplication says no matter how kids group
   numbers get the same result   kids get guilty
by association kids get   guilty   kids tear drop

decline invites for outside through the screen door
        or mama says *can't come outside & punishment*
                & loneliness multiplies hours   & mama says worry
                        multiplies every time kid sets foot outdoors
says *the wrong crowd*   but kids accumulate
next week next to Country Pantry   Lemonheads
packed in pockets   with a few coins   & Sour Warheads
        & Frooties & Fruit Chews always more kids want
always more   always more kids on the block
        always more freedom always sugar packed
in pockets always   another pocket of kids on 180th
                        another pack of bikes on Idlewild Drive
these kids divide
        when anybody's mama
                        says *get yo asses out the street*
but reassemble
        when she peels off   bike wheels crisscross
                paths   figure eight infinities on pavement

The Alchemy of Our Uncles' Chest Hair

That bounty curled from the convergence
     of shirt collar ornamented with figaro.
Sweat stagnates on the sternum,
              gilds the strands in sunlight. Our uncles
     offer a word with a Corona,
Budweiser, or Heineken in hand
     at the barbecue, chest strands snaked
over the neck of a tank top—reservoir
     for a stream of whiskey, tequila,
cognac that misses their lips,
     rolls down their chins. If you let them narrate—
       like their myths of Jameson that transmutes
into hair on our chests after the booze burns
     dull in our throats—they don't spill
       any liquor. Our uncles forget
to mention this alchemy requires patience.
     They began to manifest
       this magic in boyhood, days running the block
     with other boys until our grandmothers
       echoed their names from front stoops;
that same echo prompts the gold glow,
          summer afternoon sunlight slicked
     'round loops of our uncles chest hairs
as they turn the ribs on the grill. In their woven sandals,
       they weave their stories
     between beer sips, shots, and grown folks' conversations.
We listen to their silver-tongue tales,
     how they persuade truth to stretch
       like hair fibers spread over their collars.
     Only when their hair silvers into cuban links
do we understand how liquor can aurify
     our once-bare bodies, when we, before a mirror,
notice a single strand spirals from our chests.

Downtown Chicago, a Decadence Uncommon

Commuter train already eased into the station,
almost ready to ease out, we sprint
through the doors. Our heaves and huffs ease
to laughter staccatoed through our teeth,
then full raucous as we pick up steam,
as the train picks up steam. This cacophony
we chorus on a summer Monday morning
while conductors click tickets, work-weary
9–5'ers side-eye our upper deck chatter.
Chatter we click: jokes, favorite song lyrics
too loud for a.m. travelers, change we clink
to pay our fares, change we save for a meal
downtown. Downtown is where our skin learns
new proximities, so close sweat beads skip
from neck to neck, brow to brow. We arrive
in the Loop, still loud as locomotives
as we racket off the train, out of the station:
suburban kids bound for Gold Coast beaches,
a decadence uncommon to our shopping mall,
bowling alley, movie theater, roller rink routines
most days. Today, we grip summer like sand
—swimsuits under denim. City denizens
for the day. Lake Michigan offers its tides
to our feet, its gull-sung serenade
to our ears. Fresh water up to our chests
until the sun drops, our eyes droop. We droop
against train station columns, our gaggle
no longer giggles, just the sweat-heavy sleep
as we wait for the next train to normalcy,
as we wait for city lights to blur to black,
train cars sprinting back to the suburbs.

Black History Year

we celebrate late
winter in january
overcast grass languid skies
no snow but cold zippered chin
down feather body

snuggle
in february we praise
the cookie jar at grandma's
porcelain toad fat we reach
for more oreos

in march
when we honor minute
rice microwaved beans bubbled
slow in the stockpot mama's
cake batter whisk this turning
her hands work we never know

hunger for april we
exalt lightbulb filaments
in bloom electricity
the bill paid we do not spark
candlelight

in may we revere
our platitudes air we
offer to stifle silence
listen to stories to lies
smile all the same this mouth

june
laud sprinkler water tree seeds
box elder helicopters
cascade sun soaked saturated
kids

we dedicate july
for tying shoes walk circles
to appreciate shadows'
permanence if we could stay
daddy can fix

our tie cut
our hair by august we
laugh glorify letting go
throw roses on leftovers
faith on a dandelion

blow rippled wish september
jubilate our new blue jeans
new school year fresh we arrive
disposable our income
it grows

october we dream
fingers sunk in soil
snatch a bible and sage
resurrection a fire
of leaves the dead things

we give
gratitude in november
netflix twitter binge we scroll
the couch cushion indent
haven't considered a clock

since last december we live
complicated lives we feast
for waking up this morning
why not every syllable
celebrate?

What I Would Ask About Barack's Post-Racial White House

What manner of gospel raised Barack Hussein Obama
        on Sunday mornings in the White House, muscle memory

of mop bucket and vacuum on the Sabbath? Who awakened
        his hands? Smokie Norful? Yolanda Adams? Mary Mary?

In this hand-me-down house, spine-and-rib frames
        behind the sheetrock, how often did Barack sleep

late on a Saturday morning? Or did the voices never stop
        their whispers in his ears? I saw what he wrought

upon his soles. I imagine the dead beneath the South Lawn
        could snare a root around his toes if he did not tread

with caution. Am I asking too much of the mountain I raised
        for him? No, these questions are supposed to be for Barack,

not my illusion that on Nov. 4, 2008, we buried this country's
        history in Grant Park. We lowered it into the dirt,

threw confetti on the grave. Or so I thought, but these questions
        aren't for me. These questions are for a Black man in a tan suit

in charge of white America. Final question: Barack
        said Trayvon Martin could have been his son. In that moment,

did he know he shouldered a cross that could drag him
        back down Golgotha? It happened, but I stared at the hilltop,

and I haven't looked toward the ground since.

Just a Couple More Minutes

Vibrations signal
the first Damen Ave bus,
sunrise a clatter of gold
blades on buildings

—our southward window
a stay of amputation
for our afterglow,
alarms snoozed, snoozed,

snoozed. Foster Ave bus
nestles the curb, huffs, kneels
to admit a body. I reach
to pull your head to my chest,

grasp only blankets—shower a hush,
coffee grinder like gargled glass.

Petrichor

Rain raps the air unit: hi-hat or timpani,
        each drop drums the metal. This
percussion persists. Now thud. Now stumble.
        Now tumble into a drum roll.

This storm wails, too. What a thing to imagine,
        a scream we crave, earth with its mouth
wide, each boom a hum in the windows.
        Then the drum again. The rain eases,

each drop once more patters like an infant's
        footsteps down the hall, hands on the wall,
thunder slaps against the paint, a giggle like the sun
        peeling back storm clouds. Lightning flickers

a final goodbye. Then, petrichor,
        a memento of the storm's passing, lingers.

Sonogram

Light and murk, the sonogram
squirms. Your mother and I
  can't see you in gray. The technician

mum. Then *turn here. Press here.*
Left side now. Right side now.
  A little pressure. She can't confirm

any splotch as life. She's not qualified.
When she leaves to fetch the doctor,
  your mother is pregnant

with worry. She doesn't notice
your heartbeat blinks in the gloom.
  The doctor arrives to confirm

your beacon. In your mother's womb,
you're a crescent of light.

The American Killing Field

Charlottesville has started to fade into a "remember when?"
Boston's free speech rally will happen tomorrow.
From halfway across America, my mother warns me
to exercise caution. I tell her Massachusetts is blue.

She knows what scopes and iron sights frame Black bodies.
She watched cops choke Eric Garner on a New York street.
She watched cops shoot Tamir Rice. Rekia Boyd's killer
resigned before he could be fired. Another bullet

ricochets across America. We debate the gun smoke,
forget the trigger finger. Our mothers never lose sight
of our Black bodies down range on the American killing field
or the muzzle flash when the media murders our character.

For the gun that takes the body, they grab a graduation photo.
For what America does to us, they grab the casket lid.

pluto be orbit uncommon

i be dead   been dead   been dying   been death
god   i been a body bounce round the sun   been a body
celestial outside earth atmosphere the scientist say
at most been asteroid   say i ain't been a body
worth measure   say i got ocean beneath my skin
say my brain is full of ice   say i be cold say i be dead
say i be dead to neptune but water say life   on mars
so why i be dead   to NASA and them
school books been where i be abnormal say my axis sits
sideways seasons a mess   say i always got skin dark
skin light too   say i got wandering poles ain't no true
north atop my head   ain't no man make me wear words
for earth   i   be   orbit   uncommon   i
be   chaos   been had an orbit
upset ordinances   i be on your science magazine
methane ice glossy   halo crater scars   but i still be dead
still disposable   been body   been celestial
body be body so who gon tell me   i be   nothin
but rock who gon deny i dominate my neighborhood

Only Domestic Life

What demon troubles our home
this night? A *boom* in our apartment
wakes us. Maybe a thief?
I grab the knife I keep by the bed,

check the living room,
kitchen, bathroom, foyer,
what will be our daughter's room.
What waits for me in the dark:

bookshelf, ironing board, boxes,
bags, hoodie hanging on a door
—only domestic life. I invented
specters and burglars for each item,

for my heroics, for coming fatherhood.
The radiator pipes thunder again.

Generation Snowflake

                                                    this is how they like us
                when we float
                            down from the sky
                            when they can catch us
                                                            in their palms let the heat
                                    melt us to water
                cold a concession to enjoy
                                                    our presence they tolerate
                                only if we leave
    our ice if we lie
                                                        on the pavement
                        do not obstruct their view
                                            do not gather into banks
    on their roads do not travel
                                                    sideways they like us
                            predictable light malleable
    if they can gather
                                                several of us packed together
                into a ball they can throw
                                                    for fun that's when they like us
                            when we only powder
    their christmas   when we do not blizzard
                            or lake effect   do not accumulate
                                    more than an inch   do not grow
                into a bomb cyclone   do not rush
                                    upon them as an avalanche
    they like when they can carve us
                            with skis and snowboards
                when they don't have to bend
    their backs to shovel us
                            off their property   this is how they like us

Erosion

In my thumb & forefinger,
I roll a stone. It lost its boulder self.
I weather its geometry
to a pebble. Lifetimes carved

these angles, these faces, these edges.
Erosion shed the rock's
history: a fragment in my shoe,
a particle mixed into concrete

to build a foundation.
I toss the pebble into a pond,
where water caresses its crags.
Each new face speaks names of ages

carried on the wind like dust.
A lineage lives in each grain of sand.

How We Work This Soil

Our fingers latched to earth
to coax this country
stolen to growth. We manifested
your destiny shoulder-deep in dirt.

Our wrists anchored in soil,
we could not unhinge
our limbs from this land,
bodies prostrate for cotton

or God. You don't want testimony
of your wrongdoing. Nestled in trenches
we till, we raise the volume
on our speakers. This land hums.

Our roots steeple sidewalks.
Sage blooms in our gardens.

Exegesis on a Chicken Wing

Pull apart the flesh
between drumette, wingette.
Rip and tear the meat

with your teeth and fingers,
cheeks greasy if you eat
chicken wings the right way.

From end to end,
a linear timeline
of fat, gristle, skin

as you stretch the wing
straight. The span
from the ax to the chicken's neck

—we expect no blood
in the pan of wings from Sharks,
no reminder of sacrifice

as an exercise of hands.
Hunger is an exercise
of protest. We quell

commotion in our bellies
with mild-sauce-doused wings.
With curved acrylics,

my aunt excavates
a vein in her teeth,
sucks her canines

to loosen the carnage.
I eat chicken wings
in my campus student center

to consume familiar bones
in public. *Don't you dare*
leave all that meat

on that bone.
Suck the marrow,
gnaw the gristle

to pay respects
to those who pluck feathers,
cleave breasts from wings.

It's Ramadan. At 3 a.m.,
my roommate fries wings
to satisfy day-long hunger.

We leave a bowl of bones.
Grab a fistful; it's a register
of ancestors hunched,

elbows bent at 90 degrees,
fingers pincered
around a chicken wing.

Another bone clinks a plate.
I unhinge connective tissue.
Chicken bones scatter

in a Walmart parking lot,
on the sidewalk at Ashland and Clybourn.
In Boston Common,

another graveyard of hunger.
If I gather these remains,
I can chart a path home.

The Freedom Trail Tour Guide Shyly Mentions Slaves Were Sold at Boston Harbor

What brick would guide us   across the Atlantic?
        Ocean floor sand—this grain   was once bone, once   body.

Crispus Attucks would receive his own   branch on the trail
                from State and Congress   to Framingham
to the Harbor   to waters charted   from the Ivory Coast
                to the Americas.

Whose tax dollars would pay   for the masonry,
                                lawmakers ask. Lawmakers allege
        some history isn't worth it   to save. Ask Faneuil Hall,

the busker who beats buckets, pots, and pans—
                                first, put a few bills in his hat—
        he'll explain   where to find lineage. Check between the stone—
                        not the red   white and blue

bricks from the Common   to Bunker Hill. Time flays these streets
                to their cobbles. No family   history will sprout
if you place a seed in the pothole. You won't   heal the wound.

        Some tourists comment how nice it is that they can see remains
of times past   on the U.S.S. Constitution.   They hop
on and hop off a trolley,   stop at a bar,
                celebrate the liberties   of their bodies in waves
        of Sam Adams until the last dregs   trail down their throats.

Isaiah Bradley in Conversation with Barack Obama

I, too, gave America residence
across my skin. I held the shield
and look at its weight on my bones.
how the mantle stole my years,

how the stripes bound my fists.
branded a legend? In my dreams,
to be a symbol, the sins I hid,
like my ancestors tucked beneath

this dirt or borders that claim it.
mean nothing to my name.
off the ocean floor. I'm flesh
a mausoleum of stolen people—

kneel before its polyester,
Make a state of my body.

in my body. I draped the flag
for all of my dead brothers,
They count my grief as gray hairs,
how I cut my tongue on the stars,

And what remains of this Black man
I revisit the blood I paid
tucked into the uniform like a tie,
this soil and my feet. I don't fight to covet

A White House or monuments
I'm history you don't have to dredge
vivisected to show this country—
I'm willing to die for its freedoms,

believe I can salvage these tatters.
Pin a star to my chest. Call me captain.

Josiah X in Conversation with Barack Obama

Have you ever been free in America?   I have been free of America.
Have you ever seen God?   I have been god. The pedestal shakes
when the masses clamor for salvation,   when you're superhuman to other Blacks.
It's hard to see your reflection   when your only vantage point is

down to the ground or the barrel.   The God made of me, the God made
for me, the God made   America through the eye
of a needle: what use is faith to a hand   that rattles into a fist if I don't believe
in violence enough to punch   a keystone loose? Do I hold

the shield? I am the shield,   a symbol for white man's America.
It's never been about freedom.   I wouldn't wear the mask
or the red, white, and blue   if this had ever been about freedom.
It's about how much I can bend   the bars, how many bullets I can deflect,

how far I fall when the pedestal topples,   what devil they make of me. I disappear
when I'm no longer their hero,   when the costume starts to wear my body.

Sam Wilson in Conversation with Barack Obama

Another old white man tires
like a weapon, liberty slung on his back
chest puffed, eyes to the sky.
slumps his stature. He bestows

into my hands. This mantle of savior
as if my wings never took flight.
as this metal launched into a mouth?
from the stars and stripes

to me? The sentinel of liberty,
avenger, more American than Black
when I take up this shield—
when the next skyscraper collapses.

confine my body in red, white, and blue,
stand upon the rubble, head high,

of his office. He threw America
so he could pose, hands on hips,
Now the chainmail of his wars
the shield and a world on fire

as if I didn't already have a name,
How many teeth shattered
How much blood did he rinse
before he conscripted his burden

captain: these monikers don't make me
in America. I know this history
that I am expected to save everyone
When I wear his costume,

I must emerge from his remnants,
the latest shield for America.

Bridge Strike on Storrow Drive

Metal touching metal,
gnarl me into wreckage, shear my scalp from
                my skull as we collide. My
sides bulge then break. All my
                cargo scatters beneath
this bridge so sudden: my produce
                crates, bed that
slept in many apartments, now
debris on Storrow Drive. This overpass—
                        why do I always
                bring the fire to your I-beams?
Smoke and oil, lights and
                sirens, congestion and car horns.
        I don't interrupt
traffic flow just to mar your paint.
                        I like your graffiti
more than clearance
        signs. You hover
                        over space where rain
stops for a moment; your shadow
        could embrace my side view
                mirrors. Look,
you are the bridge.
        I am the truck,
                foot to some floor, still
heaving as a heavy thing does. I
                race to crash. These many Septembers
when my metal met your
                        metal, guts and gears
        swept to the shoulder. Not the
collision or clash; it's my hoping
each time, if even for seconds, that
                I'll coast under your steel, that
you will be my shelter.

25

Murmuration of Starlings

A murmuration of starlings like a storm cloud
—an oscillation of black, a pulse of black,
a back-&-forth of black, a throb of black.
Starlings swoop & dive in formation,
shudder left, rudder right, upward sputter,
downward drill. A specter of itself every moment,
the murmuration here, then there, then shadow,
then not. A whisper's
namesake, these starlings wind, make wind.
They woosh, fill sky with static, rip twilight black.
A body black, a body bird, a body
full of flight, the starlings speckle then splotch;
if a murmuration has enough birds—more bellow than murmur,
more wail than whisper—starlings eclipse the sun.

Sonogram

And this is a hand. What fist will you devise?
For playground bullies, a weapon?
      For the weak, to wage your own wars?

Open, raised for police, pistols drawn?
      Closed, raised for pride
in your Blackness? Interlocked, tenderness

between loved ones? *Here's the other hand.*
      Look, she's waving hello!
You already know how to invent reassurances.

What will you invent when you hold blocks?
How quickly will your hands turn wrecking ball?
      I pray, my hands together. I hope

to open them, find joy in my palms,
your tiny fist clasped around my finger.

the bees rebuild

today we build a new home,

                                        the old hive foam-smothered

                    —bodies dropped, writhed—

but today, new honeycombs

to nest our young, collect honey

                                —some twitched

          for days. we move on, restart

—dandelions bloom. everything

                              burned last time. everything

fluorescent in sunlight. we

rebuild today. we gather pollen

                            —before that, it was a hose.

         we sting. yes, we sting. we sting

              only once, only carefully.

                    we know we will die

                        if we sting.

                          they swat. we sting.

today we build a new home—

                if we can save what we love,

                    what is death?

                    we sting.

      some days, on peony petals,

we nap because we are tired.

                    we tire of how they swat. we sting

to protect—

                maybe if we didn't sting.

                maybe if we didn't fight—

                    we sting,

but only to protect the hive.

                              last time, everything burned,

                              but not before they scraped honey

              from our home.   some bodies

      burned—today we restart. today we

rebuild our home.   at sundown, what poison
                                               will douse these honeycombs?
                                               what fire—

         what else can we do but sting?

If You and Your Best Friend Don't Argue Like This at 3 a.m. in Someone's Basement, You're Not Best Friends

How Diddy have more money than Jay-Z?

                                         Diddy been had more—

How nigga? How? How he have more money?

                                           Well, if you'd listen—

Nig–ga–how–does–Did–dy–have–more–mon–ey?

            Syllables pace with clapping hands,
            a slap with each unit, a show of force.

                  Right here. Forbes. Diddy been had more money.

            The kickback down to the final dregs
            in plastic cups, our liquor-swollen words
            fumble for coherence. We crash into
            semantics. This is how we show love.

OK, that's net worth, not liquidity. What about—

                  What about nothing, nigga. You just wrong.

I–57 to Dan Ryan Improv

I–57 to the Dan Ryan / grooved
        surface fills heads with nods / thumps
    car wheels at pavement / lips jackhammers *right on*
        and gravel / grit gospel

at 159th backhoe arm waves to god / but don't it be hell
that bakes this summer / bends these lanes
      serpentine bedevils / rush hour congregations

nah, at 127th it be jazz exhaust / sputter trumpets
that get down 'round / traffic cones / that bump clink
    beat / when treads trespass / your E-T-Ayyyy / hey now
        high-vis vest and flashing / lights at 115th

      that *thunk-a-thunk-* / *a-thunk-a-thunk*
snow brush bump in the trunk
    gravel jump / all night under floodlight
          ain't no broken axle

nah, at 95th that be cars slapping / drums that *boom-da-boomp*
      that *doom-boom* / *boom-boom*
    but don't they lay it down / asphalt smooth

before that crossfade into winter / chill
        tire *skkkkiiiiiirrrrrtttt* / sudden stops
    cha cha / slide on ice
snowplow / hoedown slow down / slippery conditions
    rock salt / chatter pothole percussion

Obama's Tan Suit

button-down shirt   our mothers cinched
around necks years ago   we outgrew the yokes
tie clipped behind the collar   pant hems retreated
from payless oxfords and our only suit   only the baptism
then take it off   put it back on the hanger
so it doesn't wrinkle   only a little big in the sleeves
only a coffee stain   that should come right out
dry-cleaned   only once a year if even   only a rental
only job candidate without one   only Black
·job candidate   only the first in-person interview
                    only borrowed from our fathers
only borrowed from our uncles   only without matching
slacks and jacket   only obama in a tan suit   color after black
charcoal and navy preempt our budgets   tan a hue reserved
for summer and disposable   income   imagine
that the suit we wear   for our cousin's wedding
doesn't have to look   good enough for our funerals
that our families could bury us   in our favorite colors
tailored waist   jacket that doesn't parachute
our bodies   a suit we don't have to grow
into over time only to outgrow after only one use
only a tan suit   why not purple or burgundy why not
velvet and rhinestones   why not something bootsy
or james or little richard or prince would don   a hue
that hides stains   where we can finally spill our cognac
play our music   dance our dances   let our skin
sweat through   the fabric   on our lapels
we too could pin america

Curse of Ham

In the beginning, God created the heavens and earth
and light and sky and land and seas and vegetation
and sun and moon and fish and birds and Adam
and Eve and sin and civilization and vengeance,

and then there were curses and Black bodies:
vassal and vessel for demons of a foreign God.
We witnessed the Father's nakedness—earth He
razed. In His image, but we carried legions of devils

into the sea. I give this same God residence
on my tongue. Or is it Satan? What kneels me
to pray to His blue eyes and blonde curls,
He whose curses bruise me brown

before His white face? I grapple with revelations;
trumpets herald my doom. I kneel before a cross ablaze.

Sugar Tells a Truth About Tradition

Like when I held fistfuls of Pixy Stix, bit off the tips, guzzled sugar,
but not more than the murmur of granules dumped into Kool-Aid,
an inch of white settled on the bottom. Dare I ask my cavities
how many Fruit Chews and Frooties did I secret in pockets during school,

much like the Mary Janes my mother devoured? Don't you know that sugar
once cost a penny a piece: saltwater taffy, Smarties, Bit-O-Honey, Tootsie Rolls,
Bazooka, Brachs, Bottle Caps, caramels, sugar cigarettes. Consider sugarcane fields
around Vacherie and New Orleans, where my mother's parents tasted the sweet

they would eventually store in a jar: fun-size Snickers, Milky Ways, Hershey's
for when they needed a bit of sugar to balance out the work of the insulin
injections, my grandmother secreted away in her room, my grandfather's
fingers pricked before breakfast to check his blood sugar, my mother's

fingers pricked—the blood writes a record of relatives,
syringes stabbed in thighs. The sugar swells my waist.

Do We Need More?

Our apartment is full of trash bags
pregnant with old possessions to donate.
To make room for our daughter,

a child four months from this world,
we discard impulse buys, wedding gifts
unopened. *Do we need these goblets?*

When will we use candlestick holders?
For the clothes we haven't worn in months,
we fluff another garbage bag for Savers,

where we drop off our old belongings.
We search through other's old belongings:
onesies, sleepers, gowns. *Do we need more*

sizes? We don't know. Back at home, we sit
in her empty room. Even the dust is gone.

Passage

We are bodies
against bodies,
sweat-pearled
skin. We, cargo
of rush hour
stowed in this train,
rock in an ocean
of coughs, hot breath.
I don't complain
out loud; hurricane
crowd at Arlington,
rain-slicked umbrellas
—we jostle. We jockey
for space. We just want
to get home, to reclaim
air around our noses.

               How can that man cry in a place like this?
He bares his ruin
like wreckage at sea.
What if, at Copley,
I take his hand,
wipe red from his eyes?
      What if we leap
            over the threshold,
               onto the platform
to drown in waves
of Comm Ave brownstones?
What do I know of such freedom?

Samuel L. Jackson's "Motherfucker"

We *motherfucker* / like every syllable riddles flesh / with a new opening. We *motherfucker* / with the fury of mothers / who would slap the brown / off our skin if they heard us utter, / slap our speech to stutter. We *motherfucker* / again with friends to free our speak, / unleash phonemes garbled in our teeth. / We *motherfucker* / at school. We *motherfucker* / in the streets. We *motherfucker* / when the DJ lays down the beat. We *motherfucker* / when we won't lay down the beef / or simply because we need more punctuation / to tell you *motherfuckers* / we don't need to doublespeak. / Yes, we know *English motherfucker,* / all the ways air erupts from our throats / for scholarly quotes and polite conversation. / But what we're sayin' *motherfucker* / is when God gave us a bounty of words, / we made a meal of fricatives, nasals, and plosives / so we could flick explosions / off our tongues every time / we shout *motherfucker.* / Our grandmothers ate chitlins. / What makes you think we can't recondition / expletives for all modes of expression? *Motherfucker,* / *we eat everythang* and regurgitate / gold from our innards when we cuss. Trust / *motherfucker.*

The Stolen People Do Decree

To reclaim everything—
   from the sun
        to the screen door
slapped shut, grandmothers
who could run after us
to put a paint stick to our asses
if we acted up, roses thrown
         on too many graves, names
we earned on the block with friends

—we woke up this morning.
If you not familiar, vacate
      strongholds behind our eyes.
   Surrender any plunder

to the pot. We simmer this offering,
   spit it to dirt. Cathedrals sprout.

Reynolds-Wrapped Leftovers

casserole dish room-temp memory
          half-eaten aluminum I
clatter off the roll crackle over
      leftover meals peaks valleys crinkles
hems smoothed over the
          pyrex serving pan lip
      baked macaroni or peach cobbler
cobbled armor jagged ridges
          lunchbox sandwich sheath
      sheets sheets sheets shimmer
sheets spun round cardboard swords
          for halloween tin-man trappings
             chrome sphere cocked back
arced free throw basketball
          trash cookie crumb collateral
damage I pull too much
          try to rewind it around the roll
             now wrinkled again I pull
      sheet zippered against sharp waves
ripped like skin when a thumb
          knicks the cutter uneven tear
extra shrapnel fistfuls fragment carnage
      clutter loose scraps
kitchen drawer stuffed save
      a morsel rough edge like an old
          bulova watch retirement
gift for my grandfather's
          years at reynolds metals company
the mccook plant engraved
      on the case his grave the gun salute
my uncle places
          the watch in my palm so I can save
a piece of his father for later

Faith in the Father

My wife can feel our daughter's hiccups.
She asks if I, too, can feel the ripples.
By faith alone, I know my daughter

grows in the womb—these tremors
I cannot sense. I must believe
like I believe in God. She counts kicks,

the time between kicks. I question
the Lord's lack of obvious signs
of divine intervention

when the news announces
another body count. Our daughter
hasn't thrown a jab in some hours;

my wife places my hand on her abdomen.
Is this the time to call the doctor?
Is this the time to lose faith

in miracles? The baby stirs. I fold
into prayer, whisper to my daughter
a wish that I will soon see her face.

At the Baggage Claim, I Collect Myself

The alarm grunts its caution. The carousel revolves. We nominated our strongest warriors to represent us and form a shoulder encirclement. Into the fray, the conveyor spits luggage: black, black, blue, black, red, gray, black, purple, Spider-Man, black. We lack names. We identify ourselves with mementos affixed to suitcases: bandanas, bows, ribbons, pom poms. We, who offered ourselves to the belly of our winged god. We: flight from Orlando. We: carousel 8. Our language: sighs and groans. We launch ourselves, yank our belongings from the collective. I am black roller bag. I am plush keychain. I carry on after I collect my baggage, roll away with my life.

When I Grew Homesick for Boston Instead of Chicago

The Dan Ryan's southside start just before 87th Street:
a throat where cars fly in from I–57 and I–94, clutter

like Garrett's Popcorn kernels. That commuter cluster
unlike the Leverett Connector stop-and-go jockey for position,

the Pike's syrup drip next to Storrow Drive. Even still, I arrive
at contentment; I no longer search for a Wicker Park gait

in an Allston rat. Chicagoland's plump boulevards
can't compare to how Boston streets straddle

cars in one-ways so narrow you won't breathe. This compact
metropolis—Brookline in the crook of Boston's arm

unlike how Evanston latches onto Chicago—
makes a home in me like a rafter of turkeys that roosts

near the C Line on Beacon Street. I settle
to the point that I do not mistake a creak in my bones

for a Brown Line train as it corners in the Loop.
I do not abandon memories of Chicago summertime

carnivals that illuminate Marshfield Plaza, spill neon on I–57.
Chicago won't let me forget: my cheeks wind-scored

whenever I return home, a vortex shoved in my nostrils
to steal my words before I can speak ill of the cold.

And what does Boston gift me? Autumn and Commonwealth
Avenue in Brighton: at the top of the hill, I see a fire-lit tree

border around the city—nature's caution of old life's proximity,
the once-was always burning within reach.

Delayed MBTA Train Home as Jimi Hendrix's Stratocaster

Third rail hums electric—a rumble

       in the concrete throat. Train a stop away, delayed

for 11 minutes. *Makes me wanna get up and scream*

       —tired feet and all. Sleep-heavy head nods

after crosstown traffic navigation to Park Street,

       after long workday. The next train to shoes off,

clothes off, mind off is now approaching.

       Train cars groan around the bend, then rasp
while Jimi's *Purple Haze* riffs in my headphones.
       Ten red-striped cars thunder
the platform—steel-glass blur slingshot
      along the rails. A screech rips the station

as the train slows to a halt. In my ear canal,

       metal-on-metal grind as Jimi engraves his initials.

"I'm OK"

I'm—

the sun might scorch the earth
before I live to see retirement,
                if first the oceans don't gnaw the coasts.

this morning, i drank my coffee
                         slow. i drank my coffee
to drink my coffee, not to wake up.

my uber driver asked
where i was going,
why i was going.
                   why was i going?
have you ever stopped,
removed your socks & shoes,
waited until your toes
grew roots, fastened yourself
to the earth? i answer
enough to be conversational,
not enough to reveal
       my identity. i won't remember
       his name, just his sincerity
           —memory lingering like candle smoke.

i paid a bill & another bill
& another bill & another
bill & another bill & another bill.

                      if i sit by the window, i can feel
                        the breeze. the shades clack;
                sunlight flickers across my notebook.

i'm not, but it's impolite to tell you.

my baby daughter fell asleep
in my arms. i fell asleep.
her hand wrapped around my finger.

have you ever heard
wind rustle branches
& noticed the sound
is akin to rushing water?

racist comments on the internet: some say they're not real
        racists, just edgy teens. is there a difference?

a robin zipped into our bushes.
amidst the leaves & shadows, its chest
a flame, the bird bobbing from branch to branch.

i thought about killing myself today.
i thought about killing myself today.
i thought about killing myself today.
i thought about killing myself today.
i thought about killing myself today.
i thought about killing myself today.
i thought about killing myself today,
                but i didn't.

are you really asking,
                or is this just small talk?

if you drive into boston down route 2,
through arlington & belmont & cambridge,
you can see the skyline. at sunset,
the buildings glow
like an inferno on the horizon.

—OK. How are you?

Terror Management Theory

To measure humanity's purpose
in hungers and funerals, count
divots in the bark of an oak
tree. The voids collect

raindrops, nestle the beetle
and the worm. In the hollows
that litter our peripheral
vision, measure humanity

as the depth of a stomach
or the depth of a grave.
I want to believe everything
tossed in a hole hits a bottom.

When another body greets the earth,
I try to ignore the silence that follows.

Elegy as a Room for My Dead

I try to reinvent you. A white gravestone
in a field of white gravestones: I conjure

this image instead of you. When you died,
I was asked to write an elegy for the funeral.

I didn't know how to make you from the blank page,
another cavity for the body you inhabited to fill.

Even now, nearly a decade later, I recall
the La-Z-Boy, how you left the indent

waiting for your return like the left margin
expects my cursor will come back, another foot

to raise you another foot from the soil. Row by row,
the headstones sprawl, stanzas for the dead.

Did you know *stanza* comes from Italian?
It means *room*. Let me reconstruct you

in the living room. You sit, radio on your chest,
Sox at the Cubs for the Crosstown Classic,

a Metra train roaring, then leaving. The leaving
is where I ruminate, that the room is dirt,

and the real room is a room that's empty
of you for almost a decade now.

How much have I reinvented you in this poem
versus rendering your absence in stanza breaks,

each return another reach just short of heaven?
Over which ocean will I scatter these ashes

I wrote for you? I can't even properly visit
your headstone in a poem.

Sonogram

You look more human;
you already know to run
to free yourself.
A hokey pokey,

the technician says.
Your mother & I laugh
as she disturbs your world.
Apply pressure here. You'll forget

by the time you're born,
learn new horrors in life.
Other borders aren't kind.
The technician agitates.

You run in place, grasp & kick
these walls that make you.

all-american black body

body broke but body builds
mountain from matchsticks body
burned but body bends time
'round a wrist body bend words

worth of hurt but body writes
signs of new cancer body
crack creak shrink split rot
but rock bend low for soul

music yes my body be
flesh yes bone yes my body be
sinew yes a lot of atoms body be
adam if you ask god body be

slouched out my bed my body
is america like paper in a house fire

The Six-Eyed Sand Spider's Message to Solicitors, Evangelists, and Colonizers

I expand
my limbs,
shovel sand
onto my
body, burrow
deep, bury my-
self to be alone
with my hungers.

                        Your trespass
                   tremors my solitude.

I remain nested
in the grains,
six eyes wide,
my mandibles
venom-wet,
ready to lunge.

                   If your rhythms disrupt

my home, I will devour

                   your encroachment.
                     Martyr yourself

in my jaws
if you please. I will
emerge from isolation,
drag you into my earth.

Might Catch My Niggas

Might catch me & my niggas / knotted in the dirt: my niggas / all fists & elbows & grapples / & just a bunch of boys. / Might not say *yo mama* / again. Might not catch me / saying *nigga* in front of my mama. / Might catch my grandma / saying *nigga* in front of me. / Might catch my niggas' / chests puffed. Might catch / a brick on your forehead. / Four fingers & a thumb / might paint your eye black. Five fingers / might snatch a discount. My niggas / might catch a football. Might catch the beat. My niggas / might beef. Might not be my niggas / for long. My niggas / might mend. Might mend some shit / to gold. Might change / a dollar to a dream. You feel me, / my nigga? My nigga / you good? Might harbor some angst. Might gutter healing / in *nigga*. Like a reservoir / catches rainwater. Might catch runoff, my nigga. / Might runoff, my nigga. Yeah, might run / until they can't catch me. / Cops might snatch another Black body / with the sidewalk. Might catch pavement / in my teeth. The whole city / might catch this smoke. Might catch that brick / through a window. My mouth is glass / & cinder, & America might snatch my neck / on live TV. My life might change to a hashtag. / Might catch a bullet before I catch a break, / my niggas. Might catch a bullet / if we run. Might catch a bullet / if we don't. Might catch us before the grave.

Dave Chappelle Ponders Necromancy in South Africa
After Quitting *Chappelle's Show*

What would you do if you faced a pandemonium
of parrots who recited a spell to revive a dead man
in a dead joke? What if you realized your rot,
that you, too, are a puppet of necrotic flesh?

That spell wires your mouth and limbs
before an audience of unseen faces. A corpse
cabaret—they're too drunk on their own laughter
to notice your decay. The payment is a bandage;

the body is a wound. It's better to bed down
in soil, let time work this zombi to bones,
let these bones wither to dust to feed a root.
Let us reincarnate rather than reanimate.

Next time, let us return as leaves. Or branches
making our own laughter as we cackle in the wind.

Chicken Wing Redux

To leverage hungers and kill wasps, nail my meat
to a wooden board. Hammer it through my bone.
Place the plank over a bucket of water with a drop of soap

to break the surface tension. I beckon their hunger.
The only mouth that matters is the bucket
of water that will devour their bodies. How many drown

to eat? To live? At the dinner table, I am food.
On this board, I am death. I am salvation
for the hands that pinned me here. Leave some meat

on the bone to woo the wasps to my rot.
They whizz then sink when their wings touch water.
The dirge sounds like my bones as they splintered

against the nail, my skin dissected in your fingertips.
I was also a carcass when you held me in your teeth.

Kickback on the Moon

The moon hits me up & says it's having a kickback & says come through so I throw on a Fubu throwback & Girbaud strap jeans like they never went out of style & hop in the car & play Parliament's *Mothership Connection* on repeat with the windows down & the volume loud & I stop in Honolulu to pick up my homie on the Naval base & he steps out of the skin he has worn for the past six years & grabs the fit he wore when we were younger, you know the one with the fitted Sox cap & white-on-white Air Force Ones & he scrubs the toes with a toothbrush & that skin still fits though he has gained a little weight & I have gained a little weight & our hair lines have crawled further back on our scalps but we go & drive straight up & keep the windows down & play Janelle Monáe's *The ArchAndroid* on repeat & I don't smoke but my homie smokes & he blows an exhaust trail right through the atmosphere & we can feel the wind in our hair, even where we no longer have hair, until we can't, until we feel our bodies rise against the seatbelts & the moon calls & asks *where y'all at* & we say we'll be there in 5 mins & the moon says *niggas always late; well hurry up* & we drive until we pull up on the moon, but we don't plant a flag or our boot prints all on the ground; we take our shoes off first because that's what you do when you enter someone's home & then we see all of our favorite cousins & we shake up with the moon, who has a lake of Crown in one of its craters, who pours several handles of Everclear & fruit punch with pineapple slices in another crater, who says we can smoke in the crib if we want & I don't smoke, but my homie does & he smokes with the moon & our brothers & our sisters & our mothers & fathers & dead niggas & I don't smoke but fuck it, I smoke & the moon says *let go* so we all open our arms, spread them wide & float off the surface while Sun Ra talks about the future, while everyone is happy & smiling & we drink & sing & drink & sing & elbow-to-elbow eat fried chicken wings with black-eyed peas shelled that morning & gumbo our grandmothers had been making since that morning & they still won't share that recipe & we eat a second & third plate & fourth until the moon turns away from the sun & we rest on the dark side & sleep for a day & when the sun smacks the moon's face & wipes dusk from the moon's eyes, the moon says *we don't have to go home, but we can't stay here* & we hug goodbye & goodbye for another day, stopping to talk every time we walk a foot closer to the car & we finally get in & buckle our seatbelts & turn up the stereo again & the moon says *hold up you coming to the next kickback? The next one is on Mars.* &

My Unborn Daughter Has Nicer Furniture Than I Do

Unlike the miscellany my wife and I cobbled
together over years between apartments
—freecycled, handed down, bargain-bought—

my unborn daughter has a furniture set.
Or will have when the transaction completes.
Crib, dresser, chifforobe—all steel gray

unlike our palette of odds and ends acquired by whim
or opportunity: a table here, headboard there.
I try not to think of the price. My wife reminds me

to remove my card. The cashier glares.
The line behind us grumbles. In dollar bills,
how much of this money could I use

to build a house from a pile of cash?
The card reader bawls and bawls.

What Waves Will Carry Back to You

new water in my mouth / I rise
         as you and yours dismantle
the planet / another Starbucks
         plastic cup in my cheek /
another whale watcher
         searches for what wonders
breach my surface / I hold America's
         history in my waves /
tall ships roped at the docks /
            bodies chained at the neck /
on my tongue / British tea /
         I drank that revolution /
now commuter ferries dock
               in my teeth / I could dredge bones /
lay skulls at State and Atlantic /
           would you auction off a femur /
a souvenir for your children
         to clutch on their duck boat tour /
for now a Coke can / a plastic
               straw I spit at Rowes Wharf
a king tide / my
           waves return
             what you discard

Would-Be Rats

Brookline, dawn: squirrels note the hour
        on Pleasant Street. Squirrels
up and down tree trunks,
        in and out of trash cans
near Comm Ave. Squirrels,
        a viral tweet says, would be rats
if they came out only at night.
        Bushy tail gangs loiter:
a half-eaten apple
        in a squirrel's jaws,
two squirrels zig and zag,
        another squirrel stops and plots
the next move. I stop and stare.
        A BDP squad throws spotlight
into the morning. What dark
        do they hope to chase
from this street? Squirrels know
        the hour; though the dark
eases from the trees, daybreak
        hasn't crested the apartments.
The cops follow me
        with the light. If I roamed
this neighborhood—multi-million-dollar
        homes line these streets—
at night, what would they call me?
        They turn their attention
to the road. A squirrel bounds
        to a trash can for scraps.
The squirrel emerges,
        a banana peel in its teeth.
In my teeth, I clutch what names
        daylight affords me.

Swaddle

You stir and cry in the night,
free your arms from the blanket.
I swaddle you tighter,

rock, bounce you back to sleep.
Exhaustion sags my eyes.
You stir and cry in the night

minutes later; a fire engine wailed
and woke you. I hold you
again. I swaddle you tighter,

put you down, lay back in bed,
hope we both find sleep.
You stir and cry in the night,

your arms free once more;
you startle awake, limbs outstretched.
I swaddle you tighter,

hush your sobs to let mom rest.
I promise (you or myself?), it gets better,
even when night stirs you to cries.
I promise to swaddle you tighter.

Your Mother Says You Look Like Me

Joy bubbles up to your lips—spit bubble ripples
before you laugh, more shriek than laugh,

but this is how you can offer yourself to the world,
a world full of wonders. You haven't seen

the sphinx, the Taj Mahal, the Great Wall of China,
just my face as it crests the ridge of the couch

—my cheeks covered in yesterday's shadows,
forehead a mosaic of dry skin. You don't see ruin,

lack of moisture, a Saturday morning we slept late;
you, my baby daughter, see your life unfurl

another amazement, another magic trick to unravel
wrinkles from your brow—contortion migrated

to your mouth, a waterfall of drool, a giggle-scream.
You clasp your hands, tiny hands, shuffle your head,

flutter your legs. The undertow of your astonishment
pulls me close to your face, your eyes squinted

by your smile. You can't stop giggling,
pound your fists. My fingers strum your belly,

but it's my face, just my face that tickles you,
wriggles you with the newness of the mundane.

Before a mirror, I will agonize over my face,
every strand of hair that denies the hunger

of my razor blade. I will shape this visage for the world's
gaze, not wonder. Your stare settles to blank,

curious, a head-cocked inquisition as you study me,
then squawk again. My happy baby girl,

I miss when I could throw a sheet over my head
to create my ghosts, when I welcomed the hauntings,

when dust was a fluffle of bunnies, not decay
I shed in the corners of my waning days. You whine,

all joy dissolved in an instant, your lip curled
—a cry, a cry, a deep breath, a pause, a wail.

I whisk you into my arms, to my body; I rock
you from siren to mumble. I reinvent

the world with you, daughter, our world

where a hush in your ear can quiet all harm;
my face, once again, sparks laughter and wonder.

Wisdom on the Art of Resurrection

Eastern wind gathers ashes: a dust
devil scatters cemetery soil.
Bones awake. Listen,

end rhyme and meter expired
in our mouths. We reanimate
that pall; these dead lines grow

new flesh. We revise old magic
with an ouroboros in our fists.
Don't they know the snake

that swallows its own tail
knows the worth of its body?
To revive what became a meal

for worms, dirty your hands,
reopen graves with a golden shovel.

etymology ft. urban dictionary

after Airea D. Matthews

because my parents liked a filmmaker
or so I'm told *pulp fiction* means blood
splatter spells marvin's brain on the rear windshield
           means quentin tarantino my parents

would spell Q-U-I-N-T-I-N their own magic
          transformation but still fits in mouths
when teachers roll call or for job interviews
          but still *quentins* or *quintons* or *quentens*
when Quintin lives right there in the email handle

        google calls me *quintus* a fifth
of whiskey or lazy speakers
        who drop the *n* and *t* like *qui-in*
also rhymes with *gin* and *sin*
almost *end* but since the start begged
the universe to turn their tongues
to pronounce *in* like *inn* evict the residence

        of *e* in my name google says *st. quentin*
martyred in gaul body in a marsh
what persecution removes my head
      just a misspelling just a micro

aggression Q among friends a nickname a relic of the *i*
I try to resurrect
      urban dictionary says a princess
        called my name says big dick says *sex*
          appeal says *ultimate sex machine*
        and intimacy withheld

like the proper spelling in every birthday card
my mother still writes Quintin
until I die

    the *i* dies for *e* when a white man
  writes a bullet for my brain

    the *e* not empty nor the chamber
  urban dictionary says *empty of emotion*
but fun who writes these expectations

to my name I tried to tell you
i tried to told you
it's spelled Q-U-I-N-T-I-N
  google asks *did you mean Q-U-E-N-T-I-N*
I mean how can I voice
    these syllables my mouth
      a bloody mess

Notes

The inciting impulse for this book was when I read Joshua Jennifer Espinoza's poem "The Moon is Trans."

    The epigraph for "See What Had Happened Was" comes from Kevin Young's *The Grey Album: On the Blackness of Blackness,* published by Graywolf Press, in the chapter "The Shadow Book."

    The line "& I don't smoke, but my homie does & he smokes with the moon & our brothers & our sisters & our mothers & fathers & dead niggas" in "Kickback on the Moon" alludes to A Tribe Called Quest's song "The Space Program" off their album *We Got It from Here . . . Thank You 4 Your Service.*

    The poem "etymology ft. urban dictionary" is modeled after Airea D. Matthews's poem "etymology."

THE JOURNAL CHARLES B. WHEELER POETRY PRIZE

Claim Tickets for Stolen People
QUINTIN COLLINS

a more perfect Union
TERI ELLEN CROSS DAVIS

Praying Naked
KATIE CONDON

Lethal Theater
SUSANNAH NEVISON

Radioapocrypha
BK FISCHER

June in Eden
ROSALIE MOFFETT

Somewhere in Space
TALVIKKI ANSEL

The River Won't Hold You
KARIN GOTTSHALL

Antidote
COREY VAN LANDINGHAM

Fair Copy
REBECCA HAZELTON

Blood Prism
EDWARD HAWORTH HOEPPNER

Men as Trees Walking
KEVIN HONOLD

American Husband
KARY WAYSON

Shadeland
ANDREW GRACE

Empire Burlesque
MARK SVENVOLD

Innocence
JEAN NORDHAUS

Autumn Road
BRIAN SWANN

Spot in the Dark
BETH GYLYS